Collins

11+
English

Quick Practice Tests
Ages 10-11

Faisal Nasim

Contents

ACKNOWLEDGEMENTS

The author and publisher are grateful to the copyright holders for permission to use quoted materials and images.

p.13 'Cornish Cliffs' from *Collected Poems* by John Betjeman © 1955, 1958, 1962, 1964, 1968, 1970, 1979, 1981, 1982, 2001. Reproduced by John Murray, an imprint of Hodder & Stoughton Limited.

p.23 George Washington Biography adapted extract has been used by the courtesy of the Mount Vernon Ladies Association. www.mountvernon.org

p.33 Myths and Legends of Dragons, from: *Beasts and Monsters*, by Anthony Horowitz, © Anthony Horowitz 2010, published by Macmillan Books.

p.43 From *Life of Pi* by Yann Martel (Harcourt, 2001). © 2001 Yann Martel. With permission of the author and UK publisher, Canongate Books.

p.52 *To the Moon and Back*, by James Draven, taken from the June 2017 edition of National Geographic Traveller magazine, © James Draven, is used by kind permission of James Draven and National Geographic Traveller (UK).

Every effort has been made to trace copyright holders and obtain their permission for the use of copyright material. The author and publisher will gladly receive information enabling them to rectify any error or omission in subsequent editions. All facts are correct at time of going to press.

Published by Collins
An imprint of HarperCollins*Publishers* Limited
1 London Bridge Street
London SE1 9GF

HarperCollins*Publishers*
Macken House, 39/40 Mayor Street Upper,
Dublin 1, D01 C9W8, Ireland

ISBN: 9781844199181

First published 2018
This edition published 2020
Previously published by Letts

15 14

© HarperCollins*Publishers* Limited 2020

British Library Cataloguing in Publication Data.

A CIP record of this book is available from the British Library.

Author and Series Editor: Faisal Nasim
Commissioning Editor: Michelle I'Anson
Editor and Project Manager: Sonia Dawkins
Cover Design: Sarah Duxbury and Kevin Robbins
Text and Page Design: Ian Wrigley
Layout and Artwork: Q2A Media
Production: Natalia Rebow
Printed in India by Multivista Global Pvt. Ltd.

MIX
Paper | Supporting responsible forestry
FSC™ C007454

About this book

Familiarisation with 11+ test-style questions is a critical step in preparing your child for the 11+ selection tests. This book gives children lots of opportunities to test themselves in short, manageable bursts, helping to build confidence and improve the chance of test success.

It contains 29 tests designed to develop key English skills.

- Each test is designed to be completed within a short amount of time. Frequent, short bursts of revision are found to be more productive than lengthier sessions.

- GL Assessment tests can be quite time-pressured so these practice tests will help your child become accustomed to this style of questioning.

- We recommend your child uses a pencil to complete the tests, so that they can rub out the answers and try again at a later date if necessary.

- Children will need a pencil and a rubber to complete the tests as well as some spare paper for rough working. They will also need to be able to see a clock/watch and should have a quiet place in which to do the tests.

- Answers to every question are provided at the back of the book, with explanations given where appropriate.

- After completing the tests, children should revisit their weaker areas and attempt to improve their scores and timings.

Download a free progress chart from our website
collins.co.uk/11plus

Comprehension

You have 10 minutes to complete this test.

You have 10 questions to complete within the time given.

Read the passage and answer the questions that follow. In each question, circle the letter next to the correct answer.

EXAMPLE

Adam applauded the diver as she stepped onto the podium to collect her Olympic silver medal.

In which sport did the athlete compete?

A   Rowing

B   Gymnastics

C   Hockey

(D)   Diving

E   Football

The following is an extract from 'A Journey to the Interior of the Earth' by Jules Verne

We had started under a sky overcast but calm. There was no fear of heat, none of disastrous rain. It was just the weather for tourists.

The pleasure of riding on horseback over an unknown country made me easy to be pleased at our first start. I threw myself wholly into the pleasure of the trip, and enjoyed the feeling of
5   freedom and satisfied desire. I was beginning to take a real share in the enterprise.

"Besides," I said to myself, "where's the risk? Here we are travelling all through a most interesting country! We are about to climb a very remarkable mountain; at the worst we are going to scramble down an extinct crater. As for a passage leading to the centre of the globe, it is mere rubbish! Perfectly impossible! Very well, then; let us get all the good we can out of this
10   expedition, and don't let us haggle about the chances."

This reasoning having settled my mind, we got out of Reykjavik.

Hans, as a guide should do, moved steadily on, keeping ahead of us at an even, smooth, and rapid pace. The baggage horses followed him without giving any trouble. Then came my uncle and myself, looking not so very ill-mounted on our small but hardy animals.

15   Iceland is one of the largest islands in Europe. Its surface is 14,000 square miles, and it contains but 16,000 inhabitants. Geographers have divided it into four quarters, and we were crossing diagonally the south-west quarter, called the 'Sudvester Fjordungr'.

On leaving Reykjavik Hans took us by the seashore. We passed lean pastures which were trying very hard, but in vain, to look green; yellow came out best. The rugged peaks of the rocks
20   presented faint outlines on the eastern horizon; at times a few patches of snow, concentrating

the vague light, glittered upon the slopes of the distant mountains; certain peaks, boldly uprising, passed through the grey clouds, and reappeared above the moving mists, like breakers emerging in the heavens.

Often these chains of barren rocks made a dip towards the sea, and encroached upon the
25 scanty vegetation: but there was always enough room to pass. Besides, our horses instinctively chose the easiest places without ever slackening their pace. My uncle was refused even the satisfaction of stirring up his beast with whip or voice. He had no excuse for being impatient. I could not help smiling to see so tall a man on so small a pony, and as his long legs nearly touched the ground he looked like a six-legged centaur.

30 We were advancing at a rapid pace. The country was already almost a desert. Here and there was a lonely farm, called a boer built either of wood, or of sods, or of pieces of lava, looking like a poor beggar by the wayside.

---

1 According to the passage, which of the following best describes the weather in Iceland?

A Rainy and wet

B Dry and scorching

C Gloomy and still

D Stormy and wild

E There is no reference to the weather in the passage.

2 How did the author feel about the journey?

A He felt bored.

B He felt traumatised.

C He felt involved.

D He felt excluded.

E He felt nervous.

3 Who was Hans?

A The author

B The author's uncle

C A farmer

D The guide

E The pilot

4 According to the author, what are the characteristics of a good guide?

A He leads and moves on at a steady and regular pace.

B He waits for the other people to lead and follows suit.

C He hurries ahead at an irregular pace.

D He prefers to sit down and watch the others trek.

E He follows behind at the same pace as the slowest person.

Questions continue on next page

⑤ Why were the horses described as 'hardy'? (line 14)

  A   They hardly responded to the men.

  B   They were robust and trained to cover all terrain.

  C   Their bodies were as hard as rock.

  D   They had frail bodies.

  E   They were racehorses.

⑥ According to the passage, which of these statements is true?

  A   The passages were so narrow that they couldn't pass through.

  B   The land was very fertile.

  C   There were plenty of tourists in the country.

  D   Iceland had a small population.

  E   The guide was very lax.

⑦ How does the author describe the vegetation on the mountains by the sea?

  A   It was lush and green.

  B   It was full of thorny cacti.

  C   It was very sparse.

  D   It was dense and thick.

  E   It was marked by forests and woodlands.

⑧ How did the author's uncle look when sitting on the pony?

  A   Stately

  B   Accomplished

  C   Polished

  D   Disproportioned

  E   Regal

⑨ Which literary technique is used in this phrase?

  '…like a poor beggar by the wayside' (line 32)

  A   Simile

  B   Metaphor

  C   Hyperbole

  D   Sarcasm

  E   Idiom

⑩ Which of these is a synonym of the word 'haggle'? (line 10)

  A   Quibble

  B   Agree

  C   Beat

  D   Defeat

  E   Search

In each question, circle the letter below the group of words containing a spelling mistake.

If there is no mistake, circle the letter N.

EXAMPLE

The peeple at the festival enjoyed the party atmosphere as the moon rose high overhead.

   Ⓐ   B   C   D   N

---

(1) Gina was unsure whether the ferry could accomodate all of the passengers.

  A   B   C   D   N

(2) The shop manager had reduced all the prices to the delight of bargane hunters.

  A   B   C   D   N

(3) Ben and Lisa frequently visited the museum to explore the exhibitions and installations.

  A   B   C   D   N

(4) The young man fayled to recognise the error of his ways and was jailed for three months.

  A   B   C   D   N

(5) The mischeivous puppy enjoyed playing with both his siblings and his mother.

  A   B   C   D   N

Questions continue on next page

(6) The goalkeeper lunged desparately to his right but was unable to prevent the goal.

    A   B   C   D   N

(7) The fireman's heroic sacrafice was honoured annually by the town's residents.

    A   B   C   D   N

(8) Global sea temperatures have been rising at an acellerated pace over the last decade.

    A   B   C   D   N

(9) The award nominees were divided into various categories depending on their age.

    A   B   C   D   N

(10) My neighbour is a complete nuisance and I wish the landlord would evict him.

    A   B   C   D   N

(11) The barrister stressed to his client that she could offer no garantee of success at trial.

    A   B   C   D   N

(12) The eldest child in the large family shouldered the majority of the responsability.

    A   B   C   D   N

Score: .... / 12

Test	# Punctuation
3	You have 6 minutes to complete this test. You have 12 questions to complete within the time given.

In each question, circle the letter below the group of words containing a punctuation mistake.

If there is no mistake, circle the letter **N**.

EXAMPLE

The fireworks reflected in the thames to produce a brilliant and colourful display.

    A   **(B)**   **C**   **D**   **N**

① Henry couldnt believe what he saw. The building was disappearing before his very eyes.

    A   **B**   **C**   **D**   **N**

② Most of the cake had been eaten by Sarah and her cousins' so there was only a little left.

    A   **B**   **C**   **D**   **N**

③ George cried out, "Help! Help! Can anyone hear me!" However, he received no response.

    A   **B**   **C**   **D**   **N**

④ Fortitude grit and determination are all important traits for army soldiers.

    A   **B**   **C**   **D**   **N**

⑤ The plane was scheduled to land in paris but had now been diverted to Lyon.

    A   **B**   **C**   **D**   **N**

Questions continue on next page

6. Several of Carla's friends turned up to help; she was most grateful for their assistance.

A   B   C   D   N

7. Olivia chose to eat boiled, eggs, toast and sausages for breakfast at the hotel.

A   B   C   D   N

8. "How many guests are we expecting?" inquired Robert as he began his preparations.

A   B   C   D   N

9. Former colleagues of the deceased attended the funeral many of them brought flowers.

A   B   C   D   N

10. The pilot's application was at the top of the pile so it was the first one I looked at

A   B   C   D   N

11. "Believe me," snorted Neil, "I tried my very best to avoid coming to this establishment"

A   B   C   D   N

12. Rita didn't want to eat. However Paul and Ian were feeling absolutely famished.

A   B   C   D   N

Score: .... / 12

In each question, circle the letter below the word or group of words that most accurately completes the passage.

EXAMPLE

Finding a replacement | **change** | **chart** | **chance** | **charge** | **charger** | for her phone wasn't easy.
                        A   B   C   D   (E)

---

(1) "How many times must I ask you | **but** | **to** | **on** | **if** | **by** | remain calm?" demanded Mia.
                                      A   B   C   D   E

(2) | **Their** | **There** | **They're** | **They are** | **These** | aren't many pandas left in the wild.
    A   B   C   D   E

(3) The aircraft landed | **under** | **beneath** | **on** | **in** | **from** | top of the building.
                          A   B   C   D   E

(4) I | **not** | **have** | **was** | **had** | **being** | just finished my lunch when I heard a loud explosion.
      A   B   C   D   E

(5) Lee failed to pass the exam. | **Accepted** | **Moreover** | **However** | **Furthermore** | **Never** |,
                                   A   B   C   D   E

he was accepted anyway.

(6) She | **would** | **was** | **wanting** | **wanted** | **willing** | very much like to travel to Paris and
           A   B   C   D   E

visit the Eiffel Tower.

Questions continue on next page

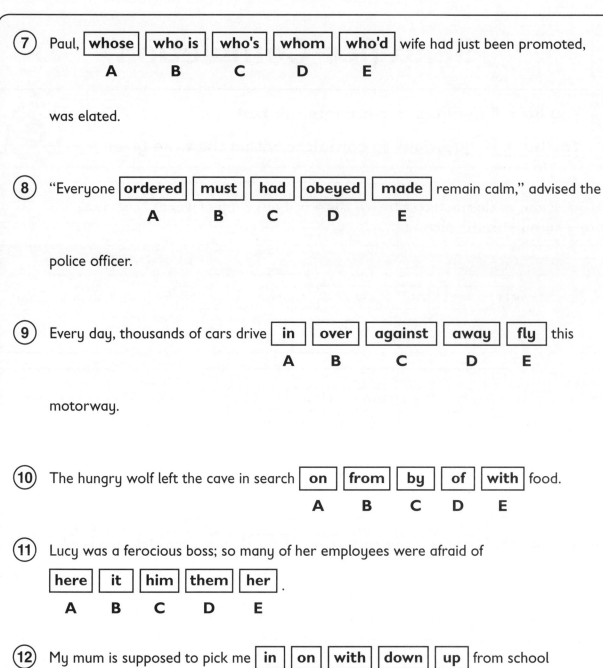

(7) Paul, **whose** **who is** **who's** **whom** **who'd** wife had just been promoted,
　　　A　　　B　　　C　　　D　　　E

was elated.

(8) "Everyone **ordered** **must** **had** **obeyed** **made** remain calm," advised the
　　　　　　　A　　　　B　　　C　　　D　　　E

police officer.

(9) Every day, thousands of cars drive **in** **over** **against** **away** **fly** this
　　　　　　　　　　　　　　　A　　　B　　　C　　　　D　　　E

motorway.

(10) The hungry wolf left the cave in search **on** **from** **by** **of** **with** food.
　　　　　　　　　　　　　　　　　　A　　　B　　　C　　D　　E

(11) Lucy was a ferocious boss; so many of her employees were afraid of
here **it** **him** **them** **her** .
　A　　B　　C　　D　　E

(12) My mum is supposed to pick me **in** **on** **with** **down** **up** from school
　　　　　　　　　　　　　　　　A　　B　　C　　　D　　　E

at 4 o'clock.

Score: .... / 12

Read the poem and answer the questions that follow. In each question, circle the letter next to the correct answer.

EXAMPLE

Adam applauded the diver as she stepped onto the podium to collect her Olympic silver medal.

In which sport did the athlete compete?

A   Rowing

B   Gymnastics

C   Hockey

(D)   Diving

E   Football

'Cornish Cliffs' by Sir John Betjeman

Those moments, tasted once and never done,
Of long surf breaking in the mid-day sun.
A far-off blow-hole booming like a gun—

The seagulls plane and circle out of sight
5   Below this thirsty, thrift-encrusted height,
The veined sea-campion buds burst into white

And gorse turns tawny orange, seen beside
Pale drifts of primroses cascading wide
To where the slate falls sheer into the tide.

10   More than in gardened Surrey, nature spills
A wealth of heather, kidney-vetch and squills
Over these long-defended Cornish hills.

A gun-emplacement of the latest war
Looks older than the hill fort built before
15   Saxon or Norman headed for the shore.

And in the shadow-less, unclouded glare
Deep blue above us fades to whiteness where
A misty sea-line meets the wash of air.

Poem continues on next page

Nut-smell of gorse and honey-smell of ling
20 Waft out to sea the freshness of the spring
On sunny shallows, green and whispering.

The wideness which the lark-song gives the sky
Shrinks at the clang of sea-birds sailing by
Whose notes are tuned to days when seas are high.

25 From today's calm, the lane's enclosing green
Leads inland to a usual Cornish scene—
Slate cottages with sycamore between,

Small fields and telly-masts and wires and poles
With, as the everlasting ocean rolls,
30 Two chapels built for half a hundred souls.

---

1 Which area is this poem about?

 A Cornwall

 B Surrey

 C Scotland

 D London

 E Essex

2 What is the following line from the poem describing?

'A far-off blow-hole booming like a gun—' (line 3)

 A A whale making noise in the distance

 B A soldier shooting a gun in the distance

 C A gust of fierce wind

 D The raging of the sea

 E The inclement weather

3 What type of reference is contained in these lines? (lines 13-15)

'A gun-emplacement of the latest war
Looks older than the hill fort built before
Saxon or Norman headed for the shore.'

 A Historical

 B Biographical

 C Scientific

 D Comedic

 E Biological

4 What is the poet describing in the following lines? (lines 17-18)

'Deep blue above us fades to whiteness where
A misty sea-line meets the wash of air.'

A   The horizon

B   The dolphins in the sea

C   The fishermen along the coast

D   The weather at the beach

E   The lush fields of the countryside

5 In which season is this poem set?

A   Summer

B   Autumn

C   Winter

D   Spring

E   Monsoon

6 Which type of birds are referenced by the poet for making the loudest sounds?

A   Carnivorous birds

B   Sea birds

C   Angry birds

D   Dangerous birds

E   Hungry birds

7 Which of these is typically found inland?

A   Wooden bungalows with oak trees

B   Slate cottages with sycamore trees between them

C   Concrete houses with banyan trees

D   Brick houses with yew trees in front of them

E   Slate cottages with mighty oak trees

8 Which of these lines from the poem suggests that the place is sparsely populated?

A   Two chapels built for half a hundred souls.

B   Saxon or Norman headed for the shore.

C   A misty sea-line meets the wash of air.

D   Over these long-defended Cornish hills.

E   Leads inland to a usual Cornish scene—

Questions continue on next page

(9) Which of the following words is closest in meaning to 'everlasting'? (line 29)

A   Temporary

B   Transient

C   Perpetual

D   Continue

E   Terminate

(10) 'Looks older than the hill fort built before' (line 14)

Which of these words is an adverb?

A   Looks

B   Older

C   Hill

D   Built

E   Before

Score: .... / 10

In each question, circle the letter below the group of words containing a spelling mistake.

If there is no mistake, circle the letter N.

EXAMPLE

The peeple at the festival enjoyed the party atmosphere as the moon rose high overhead.

(A)   B   C   D   N

---

① The business anticipated that customers would pay extra for the added conveniense.

A   B   C   D   N

② The secretery scheduled an appointment for Mr Jones to meet with the CEO.

A   B   C   D   N

③ French, Spanish and Italian are all langauges that share a number of similarities.

A   B   C   D   N

④ Try as he might, Herbert struggled to dance in rhythym with the melodious music.

A   B   C   D   N

⑤ Four out of ten of the students were pursuing a degree in Healthcare Comunications.

A   B   C   D   N

Questions continue on next page

6 Most of the audience found the man's interruptions to be rude and inconsiderate.

      A   B   C   D   **N**

7 Joe was keen to help but his contributions were rather more of a hindreance.

      A   B   C   D   **N**

8 Marvellous colours streeked across the night sky as the fireworks burst into flame.

      A   B   C   D   **N**

9 The statue occuppied pride of place in the centre of the collector's living room.

      A   B   C   D   **N**

10 The tax inspector was determined to conduct a complete and thorough investigation.

      A   B   C   D   **N**

11 The repercussions of the corrupt official's actions were disasterous for the village.

      A   B   C   D   **N**

12 A governing committee will be elected from amongst the group's founding members.

      A   B   C   D   **N**

Score: .... / 12

In each question, circle the letter below the group of words containing a punctuation mistake.

If there is no mistake, circle the letter **N**.

EXAMPLE

The fireworks reflected in the thames to produce a brilliant and colourful display.

    A   (B)   C   D   **N**

---

(1) Berlin is a vibrant and creative city that is full of artists, musicians, writers, and designers.

    A   B   C   D   **N**

(2) Do you enjoy working with your hands and building things? If so please get in touch!

    A   B   C   D   **N**

(3) The doctor peered over the rim of his glasses and bellowed, "Please enter quickly!

    A   B   C   D   **N**

(4) Wayne supported his team through the highs and the low's. He knew no other way.

    A   B   C   D   **N**

(5) Tim couldn't wait for his guests to sample his latest culinary creation; spinach ravioli.

    A   B   C   D   **N**

Questions continue on next page

6 So many aspiring actors and actresses arrived for the audition that they had to cancel it.

    A   B   C   D   N

7 Sonia Peterson the player's physiotherapist, declined to comment on the speculation.

    A   B   C   D   N

8 Never before had the quaint village of bootles been the subject of such intense interest.

    A   B   C   D   N

9 "No!" Implored the hapless salesman. "I will starve if you cut my commission!"

    A   B   C   D   N

10 Please arrive at Boston Station (Platform 1) ten minutes before departure.

    A   B   C   D   N

11 "You still need to travel North for many miles to reach that town," responded Ian.

    A   B   C   D   N

12 Yannick asked to purchase the following items glue, paper and a carton of rubbers.

    A   B   C   D   N

Score: .... / 12

In each question, circle the letter below the word or group of words that most accurately completes the passage.

EXAMPLE

Finding a replacement | change | chart | chance | charge | charger | for her phone wasn't easy.
            A   B   C   D   (E)

1. For those of you who wish to | be | have | took | take | taken | part, there will be a
                                  A   B   C   D   E

    special audition tomorrow night.

2. Last year, the participants | was | is | were | are | aren't | each given a book voucher
                                  A   B   C   D   E

    as a token of our appreciation.

3. My brother has a large collection of stamps, | where | wherein | in | of | whereas | mine
                                                   A   B   C   D   E

    is much smaller.

4. "We need to set | with | under | on | off | by | at sunrise to make it back in time,"
                     A   B   C   D   E

    decided the group leader.

Questions continue on next page

(5) The main advantage for both teams | **being** | **were** | **be** | **was** | **are** | an extra

                                               A   B   C   D   E

night of rest and recuperation.

(6) I should | **haven** | **have** | **off** | **of** | **having** | eaten more for breakfast. Now I feel hungry!

               A   B   C   D   E

(7) I | **having paid** | **had pay** | **paid** | **paying** | **have been pay** | for three packets of biscuits

          A   B   C   D   E

but he only gave me two.

(8) From a young age, Gerald had always believed | **in** | **against** | **for** | **on** | **about** | ghosts.

                                         A   B   C   D   E

(9) The little girl was very excited because she had never | **am** | **be** | **been** | **is** | **going** | to the

                                               A   B   C   D   E

circus before.

(10) "We | **are** | **am** | **shall** | **could** | **can** | not be attending the event as my husband is ill,"

         A   B   C   D   E

said Carla.

(11) It was a beautiful night so they decided to | **have slept** | **having been sleeping** | **sleep**

                                           A   B   C

| **slept** | **sleeping** | under the stars.

  D   E

(12) James now | **have thought** | **think** | **thoughts** | **thinks** | **thinking** | that he should try to

                    A   B   C   D   E

find a new job.

Score: .... / 12

Comprehension

You have 10 minutes to complete this test.

You have 10 questions to complete within the time given.

Read the passage and answer the questions that follow. In each question, circle the letter next to the correct answer.

EXAMPLE

Adam applauded the diver as she stepped onto the podium to collect her Olympic silver medal.

In which sport did the athlete compete?

A   Rowing

B   Gymnastics

C   Hockey

(D)   Diving

E   Football

The First President of the United States

George Washington served two terms as the American president. His first term (1789–1793) was occupied primarily with organising the new government and establishing administrative procedures that would make it possible for the government to operate with the energy and efficiency he believed were essential to the republic's future. An astute judge of talent,

5   he surrounded himself with the most able men in the new nation. He appointed his former aide, Alexander Hamilton, as Secretary of the Treasury; Thomas Jefferson as Secretary of State; and his former artillery chief, Henry Knox, as Secretary of War. James Madison was one of his principal advisors.

In his First Inaugural Address, Washington confessed that he was unfamiliar in the duties of civil

10   administration; however, he was one of the most able administrators ever to serve as president. He administered the government with fairness and integrity. 'His integrity was most pure,' Thomas Jefferson wrote, 'his justice the most inflexible I have ever known, no motive of interest, friendship, or hatred, being able to bias his decision.'

During Washington's first term, the Federal Government adopted a series of measures

15   proposed by Alexander Hamilton to resolve the financial crisis and establish the nation's finances on a sound basis, concluded peace treaties with the south-eastern Indian tribes, and designated a site on the Potomac River for the permanent capital of the United States. But as Washington's first term ended, a bloody Indian war continued on the north-western frontier and this posed a great threat. These problems limited the westward expansion to which

20   Washington was committed.

Passage continues on next page

Growing bias within the government also concerned Washington. Many men in the new government including Thomas Jefferson, James Madison, and other leaders of the emerging Republican Party were opposed to Hamilton's financial programme. Washington despised political bias but could do little to slow the development of political parties.

25 During his first term, Washington toured the northern and southern states and found that the new government enjoyed the general support of the American people. Convinced that the government could get along without him, he planned to step down at the end of his first term. But his cabinet members convinced him that he alone could command the respect of members of both budding political parties. Thomas Jefferson visited Washington at Mount Vernon to
30 urge him to accept a second term. Although longing to return home permanently, Washington reluctantly agreed.

Washington's second term (1793–1797) was dominated by foreign affairs and marred by a deepening bias in his own administration. Washington assumed the presidency on the eve of the French Revolution, a great international crisis. The outbreak of a general European war in 1793
35 forced the crisis to the centre of American politics. War would be disastrous for commerce and shatter the nation's finances. The country's future depended on the increase in wealth and opportunity that would come from commerce and westward expansion. One of Washington's most important accomplishments was keeping the United States out of the war, giving the new nation an opportunity to grow in strength. Although Washington's department heads agreed
40 that the United States should remain neutral, disagreements over foreign policy provoked tensions among them.

Despite Washington's disappointment with the rise of division in the party, the last years of his presidency were distinguished by important achievements. The long Indian war on the north-west frontier was won and many more hurdles were removed. These achievements opened the
45 west to settlement. Washington's farewell address helped to summarise many of Washington's strongest held beliefs about what it would take to sustain and grow the young nation that he helped found.

1. Why was Washington successful as a president?

A He was a very rigid, partial and egotistic leader.

B He influenced the law to favour his friends and family members.

C He was a staunch supporter of communism and favoured radical decisions.

D He surrounded himself with able administrators and was known for his integrity.

E His foreign policies were unfavourable and this helped America develop as a nuclear country.

2. Who was one of Washington's chief advisors?

A Thomas Jefferson

B Alexander Hamilton

C Henry Knox

D James Madison

E None of the above

(3) What was the main threat towards the end of Washington's first term?

A   There was an Indian war on the south-eastern frontier.

B   There was an Indian war on the south-western frontier.

C   There was an acute water crisis.

D   There was a severe financial crisis and an unstable economy.

E   There was an Indian war on the north-western frontier.

(4) What was one consequence of differences within Washington's party?

A   There was a huge rally on the south-western frontier.

B   New political parties started to mushroom.

C   The party was unable to cope with the economic crisis.

D   More peace treaties were signed.

E   Washington had to retire from his tenure as the president.

(5) What happened at the end of Washington's first term?

A   He longed to go back home but his aides persuaded him to pursue a second term.

B   He was very eager to embark on a second term as the president.

C   He was keen on a second term, but his aides didn't favour his return to power.

D   He was ready to retire and his aides agreed that he needed a break from politics.

E   A new leader had already been elected to become the next president.

(6) How did an international crisis make Washington's job tougher?

A   An international crisis yielded a better economy and a more stable government.

B   An international crisis always affected only the country in which it happened.

C   An international crisis shattered the economy and finances of the country because of disruption in trade and commerce.

D   An international crisis prevented people from travelling to the country that was affected by the crisis.

E   An international crisis caused global drought.

(7) Which statement is true about Washington's second term?

A   It lasted for a decade.

B   The world was free of major crises.

C   It was affected by foreign affairs.

D   His own party remained very impartial.

E   The US became heavily involved in European conflicts.

Questions continue on next page

(8) Which genre best describes this passage?

A Fiction

B Fable

C Thesaurus

D Scientific

E Biography

(9) What types of words are these?

programme (line 23)   problems (line 19)   administration (line 10)   people (line 26)

A Abstract nouns

B Proper nouns

C Common nouns

D Pronouns

E Verbs

(10) 'Despite Washington's disappointment with the rise of division in the party, the last years of his presidency were distinguished by important achievements.' (lines 42–43)

What is the meaning of the word 'distinguished' as it is used in this sentence?

A Marked

B Separated

C Prominent

D Illustrious

E Decided

Score: .... / 10

Spelling

You have 6 minutes to complete this test.

You have 12 questions to complete within the time given.

In each question, circle the letter below the group of words containing a spelling mistake.

If there is no mistake, circle the letter **N**.

EXAMPLE

The peeple at the festival enjoyed the party atmosphere as the moon rose high overhead.

(A)   B   C   D   N

---

① The journey back home proved to be very awkard for all the vehicle's passengers.

A   B   C   D   N

② Caroline failed to make a conscious effort to rectify the serious situation.

A   B   C   D   N

③ Many species of fish will soon be extinct, meaning they will no longer be in existense.

A   B   C   D   N

④ The officer said, "It's a great priviledge to stand before you and address these concerns."

A   B   C   D   N

⑤ The council needed to purchase some more land as the cemetary was almost full.

A   B   C   D   N

Questions continue on next page

6 Frieda struggled with the pronounciation of many words in her French classes.

A   B   C   D   **N**

7 Seven cars pass through this stretch of road every sixty seconds, on average.

A   B   C   D   **N**

8 The victim exagerated the extent of the injuries he had suffered in the attack.

A   B   C   D   **N**

9 Harassment and bullying should not be tolerated at school or in the workplace.

A   B   C   D   **N**

10 A handful of politicians decided to band together and support enviromental causes.

A   B   C   D   **N**

11 The defendant felt that the twelfth jury member would be prejudiced against her.

A   B   C   D   **N**

12 The carefree and foolish man failed to apreciate the gravity of his current predicament.

A   B   C   D   **N**

Score: .... / 12

Punctuation

In each question, circle the letter below the group of words containing a punctuation mistake.

If there is no mistake, circle the letter **N**.

EXAMPLE

The fireworks reflected in the thames to produce a brilliant and colourful display.

A   **(B)**   C   D   N

---

1 The monsoon season here usually runs from late Summer to late November.

A   B   C   D   N

2 The cat's long whiskers' and glistening fur gave her quite a regal appearance.

A   B   C   D   N

3 Have you ever thought about joining the swimming club? Its great exercise and good fun!

A   B   C   D   N

4 The new employees were asked to arrive at the facility by three oclock at the very latest.

A   B   C   D   N

5 It's not reasonable to expect it all to be completed by this afternoon. Thats unrealistic.

A   B   C   D   N

Questions continue on next page

(6) "Surely you don't expect me to shop, cook, and clean?" demanded the incredulous nurse.

    A   B   C   D   N

(7) All of the man's clothes' had been burnt in the fire and so he had nothing left to wear.

    A   B   C   D   N

(8) The journey took them almost all of wednesday to complete so they arrived exhausted.

    A   B   C   D   N

(9) Imran asked the astronaut, Can you describe what it feels like to float in space?"

    A   B   C   D   N

(10) Only three boys and four girls managed to complete all of the teachers' exercises.

    A   B   C   D   N

(11) All of the knight's opponents – and there were many of them – gathered in the square

    A   B   C   D   N

(12) Hugh and Emma queued up to buy tickets for their favourite musical, 'the Lion King'.

    A   B   C   D   N

Score: .... / 12

In each question, circle the letter below the word or group of words that most accurately completes the passage.

EXAMPLE

Finding a replacement | change | chart | chance | charge | charger | for her phone wasn't easy.
                       A   B   C   D   (E)

① Bruno | is | is going | went | goes | go | to the archive last week to do some research.
       A   B   C   D   E

② My brother didn't agree | with | for | at | on | by | me and so we discussed the issue for
                        A   B   C   D   E

some time.

③ The car, | that's | it | those | which | witch | weighed around 500 kg, was too heavy to
           A   B   C   D   E

be lifted by one person.

④ Several of the boys | are | went | where | is | was | going to the cinema this evening.
                A   B   C   D   E

⑤ The elephant that I saw was not the one | them | those | what | that | whom | caused
                                   A   B   C   D   E

this damage.

Questions continue on next page

31

(6) " **Weer** **We're** **Where** **Were** **Wear** aiming to arrive around 8 o'clock,"
     A   **B**   **C**   **D**   **E**

said Henry.

(7) The team's new player was as strong **in** **by** **as** **than** **then** an ox.
                             A   **B**   **C**   **D**   **E**

(8) All of the town's citizens wished the mansion was **they'res** **their** **there's**
                                           A   **B**   **C**

theirs **theres** .
  D   **E**

(9) "Don't **stood** **standing** **is standing** **to stand** **stand** up!" cried the angry
       A   **B**   **C**   **D**   **E**

barrister as he shuffled through his notes.

(10) Ruth objected **to** **for** **with** **from** **in** the treatment she had received from the
                A   **B**   **C**   **D**   **E**

customer service agent.

(11) The man responsible for the mess **implore** **imploring** **implorer** **implored**
                                 A   **B**   **C**   **D**

had been implored the others to keep it a secret.
       E

(12) Victor had been accused **between** **of** **by** **in** **from** theft but he swore that he
                          A   **B** **C** **D**   **E**

was innocent.

Score: .... / 12

Read the passage and answer the questions that follow. In each question, circle the letter next to the correct answer.

EXAMPLE

Adam applauded the diver as she stepped onto the podium to collect her Olympic silver medal.

In which sport did the athlete compete?

A Rowing

B Gymnastics

C Hockey

D Diving

E Football

The following is an extract from 'Beasts and Monsters' by Anthony Horowitz

There are no dragons today – mainly thanks to the knights and heroes who so thoughtlessly rode about the place killing them off. This is a pity, for dragons must have been astonishing creatures; part snake and part crocodile, with bits of lion, eagle and hawk thrown in for good measure. Not only could they leap into the air and fly but they could also run at great speed.
5   Not that a dragon would ever run away. Dragons were generally very brave creatures. When they were angry or frightened, smoke would come hissing out of their nostrils. When things got really rough, flames would rush out of their mouths. But there was no such thing as a cowardly dragon.

Only the Chinese understood and admired the dragon. It was often said that some of the
10   greatest Chinese emperors had been born the sons of dragons. Dragon bones and teeth were used as medicine. A dragon guarded the houses of the Chinese gods and brought rain to the earth when the crops needed it. That is why the Chinese still fly dragon kites and honour the dragon by including paper models of it in their New Year celebrations.

In the east, the dragon was by turns deity and demon; carried westward, it fell almost wholly
15   into the latter estate and has been transformed more recently into a purely allegorical figure. It has its counterpart, if not its descendants, in the religious faith and rites of every known land and all sorts of peoples.

Passage continues on next page

One legend has it that six to seven thousand years ago, when living conditions were extremely harsh, the early Chinese believed that certain species of animals or plants possessed the power to overcome nature's fury. Different tribes regarded a particular animal or plant as their totem, a tribe's special guardian able to provide food and avert disaster through omens or signs. At that time, there were great numbers of tribes scattered all over China, each worshipping its own totem. Among them was a tribe located in Central China, on the middle and lower reaches of the Yellow River, which used the snake as its totem. They called the snake "dragon" and owed their victories in battle to the dragon's protection. Whenever they conquered another totemic tribe, they added part of that totem to the snake to show that they had annexed another tribe. For example, when they annexed the tribe with a deer totem, the deer's antlers were added to the head of the snake. In this way, the dragon finally became the creature of *Nine Resemblances*: head of a camel, horns of a deer, eyes of a hare, ears of a bull, neck of a snake, belly of a clam, scales of a carp, claws of an eagle, and paws of a tiger. Additional descriptions added whiskers on each side of its mouth, the voice of a copper gong and lethal scales which were reversed under the throat and extended out 12 inches. A later scholar described this dragon of nine resemblances as having nine rows of nine scales each. Nine is an important and lucky number in China. A large white pearl, often shown in the dragon's claws or jaws, was its most precious possession. The pearl gave off a radiant light which never faded and was the source of the dragon's power.

The dragon holds a central role in Chinese myth and legend. It was identified as one of the four benevolent spiritual animals, the symbol of all things male. The second was the phoenix, the symbol of all things female. The other two were the unicorn and the tortoise. After the creation of man, Tien Ti, the Emperor of Heaven, observed the wickedness of man and sent a flood which covered most of the land. Yu, a younger god, took pity and asked for man's forgiveness. With Tien Ti's permission, Yu descended to earth with a giant black tortoise carrying magic soil to absorb the flood and an emerald-scaled dragon whose wings he used to sculpt the land. For thirty years, he travelled the earth scattering the soil and using the dragon's tail to carve out the steppes, mountains, rivers and valleys of China.

(1) What attitude did knights and heroes have towards dragons?

  A They were considerate and selfless towards dragons.

  B They treated dragons sympathetically.

  C They were extremely caring and compassionate towards dragons.

  D They were disinterested in dragons.

  E They viewed dragons as an enemy.

(2) What did dragons do when they were scared?

  A They ran away.

  B The leapt into nearby fields.

  C They hissed smoke out of their nostrils.

  D They flew up into the air.

  E They changed their form into that of a lion.

(3) Which of these statements is false?

A   The Chinese revered the dragon.

B   Dragons were courageous.

C   In the west, people considered dragons as demons.

D   Dragons were believed to have caused drought and famine in China.

E   Dragons were considered to be the guardians of tribes in China.

(4) How do those in the west treat the concept of dragons today?

A   They mainly treat dragons as symbolic or figurative creatures.

B   They worship dragons.

C   They build temples for dragons.

D   They treat dragons as friends.

E   They believe in literal dragons and are afraid of them.

(5) What was believed to relieve people from nature's rage?

A   Plants and animals

B   Kings

C   Queens and princesses

D   Thunder

E   Knights and heroes

(6) What was a totem?

A   The king's command

B   A plan that the tribes used to conquer other tribes

C   A sacred symbol or icon that was thought to bring good fortune

D   A wicked symbol that was thought to bring bad luck

E   A tribe's army

(7) How were the wings of the emerald-scaled dragon used?

A   To ward off evil

B   To fight the conquerors

C   To appease the sinful souls

D   To carve out the terrain of China

E   To spit fire all over China

Questions continue on next page

(8) Which four creatures were benevolent spiritual animals?

    A   The dragon, phoenix, lion and deer

    B   The dragon, phoenix, tortoise and unicorn

    C   The dragon, phoenix, deer and unicorn

    D   The dragon, phoenix, tortoise and lion

    E   The dragon, phoenix, lion and unicorn

(9) Which word has a similar meaning to 'guardian'? (line 21)

    A   Fire

    B   Attacker

    C   Protector

    D   Marker

    E   Gold

(10) '...thrown in for good measure' (line 3–4)

What is the meaning of this idiom?

    A   Well measured

    B   Throwing measurements

    C   Underestimated

    D   In addition to other things

    E   Perfect measurements

Score: .... / 10

Spelling

You have 6 minutes to complete this test.

You have 12 questions to complete within the time given.

In each question, circle the letter below the group of words containing a spelling mistake.

If there is no mistake, circle the letter **N**.

EXAMPLE

The peeple at the festival enjoyed the party atmosphere as the moon rose high overhead.

Ⓐ   B   C   D   N

① The programe for the event was handed out to each of the participants as they arrived.

A   B   C   D   N

② The doctor reccomended that the patient did thirty minutes of exercise each day.

A   B   C   D   N

③ It's not my favourite restaraunt but the atmosphere is warm and the service is friendly.

A   B   C   D   N

④ The amateur dramatists eagerly waited for the curtains to draw open so they could begin.

A   B   C   D   N

⑤ The familiar aroma of home-baked brownies wafted through Sam's bedroom window.

A   B   C   D   N

Questions continue on next page

(6) "I would appreciate it if you did not interfere in my business!" cried the agrieved lawyer.

| A | B | C | D | N |

(7) Helen hoped that there was a sensible explaination for all the delays she had been facing.

| A | B | C | D | N |

(8) Thunder rolled and lightening flashed over the tiny village on the outskirts of London.

| A | B | C | D | N |

(9) Ocasionally their work is difficult and painful but it is always absolutely necessary.

| A | B | C | D | N |

(10) The judge decided that the criminal had been suficiently punished and so he was freed.

| A | B | C | D | N |

(11) If your dog continues to display aggresive behaviour, I will have to take further action.

| A | B | C | D | N |

(12) Bella practiced her new signature over and over again in her newly purchased notebook.

| A | B | C | D | N |

Score: .... / 12

38

Test	**Punctuation**	
15	You have 6 minutes to complete this test.	
	You have 12 questions to complete within the time given.	

In each question, circle the letter below the group of words containing a punctuation mistake.

If there is no mistake, circle the letter **N**.

EXAMPLE

The fireworks reflected in the thames to produce a brilliant and colourful display.

A   **(B)**   C   D   **N**

---

① The show hadnt even begun before there was a loud commotion in the crowd.

A   B   C   D   **N**

② The wall was painted in multiple colours: Green, blue, red, yellow and orange.

A   B   C   D   **N**

③ Francis leaned over the table and whispered into his ear. "I'm watching you."

A   B   C   D   **N**

④ Each plant was put in its own container and then placed into a larger square-shaped bucket.

A   B   C   D   **N**

⑤ Samantha was put in charge of organising the school's annual Winter Fair.

A   B   C   D   **N**

Questions continue on next page

6 Ji-Yun took a deep breath looked straight ahead and jumped off the diving board.

A B C D N

7 "There aren't any left," apologised the shopkeeper. "I will order more tomorrow."

A B C D N

8 The police officer's brother's wife had been operating as an undercover agent.

A B C D N

9 William's dog, who had been behaving very well received a number of tasty treats.

A B C D N

10 Simone and Alina were shocked when they discovered what was in the box — a map!

A B C D N

11 My youngest daughter graduated from the university of Oxford today.

A B C D N

12 Victoria couldn't wait to get home and spend Christmas eve with her family.

A B C D N

Score: .... / 12

40

You have 6 minutes to complete this test.

You have 12 questions to complete within the time given.

In each question, circle the letter below the word or group of words that most accurately completes the passage.

EXAMPLE

Finding a replacement | change | chart | chance | charge | charger | for her phone wasn't easy.

            A   **B**   **C**   **D**   **(E)**

---

1. Kim is a journalist who is | **known** | **knowing** | **none** | **had known** | **know** | to be firm

             A   **B**   **C**   **D**   **E**

but fair in her reporting.

2. Gregory congratulated Mike and Ian | **above** | **upon** | **from** | **on** | **in** | their

             A   **B**   **C**   **D**   **E**

wonderful achievement.

3. Constructing furniture out of wood is | **negative** | **nigh** | **no** | **not** | **never** | mean feat.

             A   **B**   **C**   **D**   **E**

4. We | **waiter** | **had waiting** | **had been waited** | **had been waiting** | **waiting** | for hours

       A   **B**   **C**   **D**   **E**

before the man finally arrived.

5. He lost his passport | **so** | **because** | **due** | **in** | **before** | he will not be able to travel abroad.

          A   **B**   **C**   **D**   **E**

Questions continue on next page

(6) The Arctic is one of the | most cold | | coldest | | most colder | | more colder |
                                           A   **B**   **C**   **D**

| more coldest | places on Earth.
     E

(7) "| Pick | | Picking | | Picked | | Picker | | Picks | that up. You must not litter!" said the
   A   **B**   **C**   **D**   **E**

teacher to the student.

(8) | Moreover | | Nevertheless | | For | | So | | Since | the shop was closed, they were unable to
    A   **B**   **C**   **D**   **E**

purchase ice cream.

(9) The gathering takes place | wherein | | prior | | within | | in | | on | the first Sunday of
                             A   **B**   **C**   **D** **E**

every month.

(10) Buster the dog eyed the chocolate cake | hunger | | hungrily | | hungry | | hungered |
                                          A   **B**   **C**   **D**

| hung | .
 E

(11) Sheena | should have | | should of | | could of | | should | | might | stopped at the red light
          A   **B**   **C**   **D**   **E**

but she did not see it.

(12) The devout lady had dedicated her life | in | | to | | for | | with | | against | helping and
                               A **B** **C** **D**   **E**

serving others.

Score: .... / 12

Test	# Comprehension
17	You have 10 minutes to complete this test.
	You have 10 questions to complete within the time given.

Read the passage and answer the questions that follow. In each question, circle the letter next to the correct answer.

EXAMPLE

Adam applauded the diver as she stepped onto the podium to collect her Olympic silver medal.

In which sport did the athlete compete?

A Rowing

B Gymnastics

C Hockey

(D) Diving

E Football

The following is an extract from 'Life of Pi' by Yann Martel

It was a huge zoo, spread over numberless acres, big enough to require a train to explore it, though it seemed to get smaller as I grew older, train included. Now it's so small it fits in my head. You must imagine a hot and humid place, bathed in sunshine and bright colours. The riot of flowers is incessant. There are trees, shrubs and climbing plants in profusion – peepuls,
5 gulmohurs, flames of the forest, red silk cottons, jacarandas, mangoes, jackfruits and many others that would remain unknown to you if they didn't have neat labels at their feet. There are benches. On these benches you see men sleeping, stretched out, or couples sitting. Suddenly, amidst the tall and slim trees up ahead, you notice two giraffes quietly observing you. The sight is not the last of your surprises. The next moment you are startled by a furious outburst
10 coming from a great troupe of monkeys, only outdone in volume by the shrill cries of strange birds. You come to a turnstile. You distractedly pay a small sum of money. You move on. You see a low wall. What can you expect beyond a low wall? Certainly not a shallow pit with two mighty Indian rhinoceros. But that is what you find. And when you turn your head you see the elephant that was there all along, so big you didn't notice it. And in the pond you realize those
15 are hippopotamuses floating in the water. The more you look, the more you see.

To me, it was paradise on earth. I have nothing but the fondest memories of growing up in a zoo. I lived the life of a prince. What king's son had such vast, luxuriant grounds to play about? My alarm clock during my childhood was a pride of lions. They were no Swiss clocks, but the lions could be counted upon to roar their heads off between five-thirty and six every morning.
20 Breakfast was punctuated by the shrieks and cries of howler monkeys, birds and Moluccan

Passage continues on next page

cockatoos. I left for school under the benevolent gaze not only of Mother but also of bright-eyed otters and burly American bison and stretching and yawning orangutans. I looked up as I ran under some trees otherwise peafowl might excrete on me. Better to go by the trees that sheltered the large colonies of fruit bats; the only assault there at that early hour was

25 the bats' discordant concerts of squeaking and chattering. On my way out I might stop by to look at some shiny frogs – glazed bright, bright green, or yellow and deep blue, or brown and pale green. Or it might be birds that caught my attention: pink flamingos or black swans or one-wattled cassowaries, or something smaller, silver diamond doves, Cape glossy starlings, peach-faced lovebirds, orange-fronted parakeets. Not likely that the elephants, the seals, the big

30 cats or the bears would be up and doing, but the baboons, the macaques, the mangabeys, the gibbons, the deer, the tapirs, the llamas, the giraffes, the mongooses were early risers.

---

(1) What was the weather like in the zoo?

A   It was freezing and icy.

B   It was bitter and chilly.

C   It was extremely windy and blustery.

D   It was hot and humid.

E   It was gusty and stormy.

(2) Which of these quotes refers to the abundant plants in the zoo?

A   '…spread over numberless acres…' (line 1)

B   'The riot of flowers is incessant.' (line 3–4)

C   'The sight is not the last of your surprises' (line 8–9)

D   '…you are startled by a furious outburst…' (line 9)

E   '…glazed bright, bright green, or yellow and deep blue, or brown and pale green.' (line 26)

(3) What are jacarandas?

A   Plants

B   Hats

C   Animals

D   Insects

E   Birds

(4) What surpassed the frenzy and sound of the monkeys?

A   The shrill cries of birds

B   The trumpeting of elephants

C   The burp of toads

D   The roar of lions

E   The croak of frogs

5) What was the purpose of the turnstile in the zoo?

    A   It was the exit from the zoo.

    B   It was to protect the zookeeper.

    C   It was for the monkeys to play with.

    D   It was a barrier to prevent entry to the zoo without payment.

    E   It was an entrance to the author's house.

6) Why do you think the author called the zoo a 'paradise on earth'? (line 16)

    A   The author had fond memories of his time at the zoo.

    B   The author was ambivalent towards his experiences at the zoo.

    C   The author did not enjoy his childhood in the zoo.

    D   The zoo was located in the skies.

    E   The zoo was as warm as paradise.

7) When did the lions roar?

    A   They never roared in the morning.

    B   They roared every morning.

    C   They only roared on certain evenings.

    D   They roared only on the days they hunted.

    E   They roared at different times each day.

8) Which animal did the author not see in the morning?

    A   Baboons

    B   Gibbons

    C   Giraffes

    D   Llamas

    E   Seals

9) What is the meaning of the word 'furious' (line 9) as it is used in the passage?

    A   Shocking

    B   Boiling

    C   Extremely angry

    D   Calm

    E   Rushed

10) What does the phrase 'benevolent gaze' (line 21) mean?

    A   Kind regard

    B   Curious examination

    C   Inquisitive ogle

    D   Wild stare

    E   Quick glance

Score: .... / 10

Spelling

You have 6 minutes to complete this test.

You have 12 questions to complete within the time given.

In each question, circle the letter below the group of words containing a spelling mistake.

If there is no mistake, circle the letter **N**.

EXAMPLE

The peeple at the festival enjoyed the party atmosphere as the moon rose high overhead.

Ⓐ   B   C   D   N

---

1 The competiton was usually held on the first Sunday of every month in summer.

A   B   C   D   N

2 The leaflet explained how members could fully enjoy the benefits of the lesiure centre.

A   B   C   D   N

3 Parlament breaks up in summer for the holidays, unless there is an emergency situation.

A   B   C   D   N

4 Acording to the study, four out of every ten Chinese citizens speak a foreign language.

A   B   C   D   N

5 "What is your proffesion?" inquired the snooty banker at Megan's dinner party.

A   B   C   D   N

6 Ed blushed with embarrassment when his mum pecked him on the cheek at the party.

A   B   C   D   N

7 The library encouraged visitors to suggest ways in which it could improve its services.

    A   B   C   D   **N**

8 Many ancient tombs and treasures were discovered by intrepid explorers in Egypt.

    A   B   C   D   **N**

9 Clare forgot to attach the document to the email before she sent it to her teacher.

    A   B   C   D   **N**

10 Strong local comunities can really help develop social cohesion within society.

    A   B   C   D   **N**

11 Fred failed to persaude Rahul to join him on his latest expedition to Antarctica.

    A   B   C   D   **N**

12 Vera dreamt of owning a small plot of land where she could grow her own vegtables.

    A   B   C   D   **N**

Score: .... / 12

Punctuation

In each question, circle the letter below the group of words containing a punctuation mistake.

If there is no mistake, circle the letter **N**.

EXAMPLE

The fireworks reflected in the thames to produce a brilliant and colourful display.

A　(B)　C　D　　N

---

(1) The soldier distributed the remaining provisions to the desperate villagers.

A　B　C　D　　N

(2) The dog trainer was extremely fond of all breeds but my favourite was the Labrador.

A　B　C　D　　N

(3) Felix quickly caught up with Sid and asked, "What do you think your'e doing?"

A　B　C　D　　N

(4) Rose closed her eyes rested her head on the grass and fell asleep within seconds.

A　B　C　D　　N

(5) The postman was accustomed to the sound of dogs' barks as he completed his round.

A　B　C　D　　N

(6) Before finishing his homework Sam sneaked out through the window to go and play.

A　B　C　D　　N

(7) Theyre all planning to go to the club after the game to have dinner and socialise.

    A   B   C   D   N

(8) Davina continued to stare in wonder at her polished gleaming, one-of-a-kind ring.

    A   B   C   D   N

(9) "There's not much time left!" wailed Cristina. "We need to act now before its too late!"

    A   B   C   D   N

(10) The woodstock neighbourhood in Cape Town is famous for its industrial heritage.

    A   B   C   D   N

(11) "I've yet to hear a valid reason to excuse your son's behaviour." stated Mrs Holder.

    A   B   C   D   N

(12) The church is slightly to the West of the park, around 200 metres beyond the station.

    A   B   C   D   N

Score: .... / 12

In each question, circle the letter below the word or group of words that most accurately completes the passage.

EXAMPLE

Finding a replacement │ **change** │ **chart** │ **chance** │ **charge** │ **charger** │ for her phone wasn't easy.

              A   **B**   **C**   **D**   Ⓔ

---

(1) Rebecca could hear the dishwasher │ **whir** │ **whirred** │ **being whirring** │ **whirring** │

                                 A   **B**   **C**   **D**

│ **having been whirred** │ in the kitchen.

        E

(2) "│ **Wasn't** │ **Isn't** │ **Was** │ **Where** │ **Weren't** │ there more than two pieces of meat in the

    A   **B**   **C**   **D**   **E**

fridge?" asked Betty.

(3) I want to exchange one of my playing cards │ **about** │ **from** │ **on** │ **for** │ **in** │ one of yours.

                                      A   **B**   **C** **D** **E**

(4) Bob had found the ideal way to escape whilst evading │ **noticed** │ **noticing** │ **being notice** │

                                            A   **B**   **C**

│ **not** │ **notice** │.

 D   **E**

(5) "How do you │ **feel about** │ **feeling about** │ **felt about** │ **felt regarding** │

                  A   **B**   **C**   **D**

│ **feeling regarding** │ that?" asked the psychologist.

       E

6 The delighted boy was informed that he could choose | **whoever** | **whatsoever** |

                                                                     A   B

| **whichever** | **wither** | **whomever** | toy he wanted.

      C   D   E

7 The quicker you finish your homework, the | **most early** | **more earlier** | **earliest** |

                                                    A   B   C

| **earlier** | **early** | you can go out and play.

      D   E

8 Mitch | **lean** | **leant** | **lent** | **leaning** | **been leant** | against the wall and flicked his fingers

         A   B   C   D   E

through his hair.

9 The young father was determined to provide | **in** | **about** | **respect** | **above** | **for** |

                                           A   B   C   D   E

his family.

10 Few | **have** | **of** | **or** | **off** | **for** | the remaining passengers were awake at the time.

         A   B   C   D   E

11 We will begin | **promptly** | **prompted** | **prompt** | **prompter** | **promptest** | so please

                  A   B   C   D   E

ensure you arrive on time.

12 | **Furthermore** | **Regarding** | **Nevertheless** | **If** | **Moreover** | Derek did not manage to

         A   B   C   D   E

catch the train, he would have to walk home.

Score: .... / 12

Comprehension

Read the passage and answer the questions that follow. In each question, circle the letter next to the correct answer.

EXAMPLE

Adam applauded the diver as she stepped onto the podium to collect her Olympic silver medal.

In which sport did the athlete compete?

A   Rowing

B   Gymnastics

C   Hockey

(D)   Diving

E   Football

The following is an extract from 'To the Moon and Back' by James Draven; *National Geographic Traveller* magazine

It's a frosty 6 am and the sun is peeping over the mountainous horizon. Just as its warming rays bloom against the skyline, our aircraft sinks below the edge of its launch pad – a sliver of canyon cliff – and the sun disappears behind the peaks again. This is the first time I've ever descended at take-off.

5   This is also the first time the pilot has freely admitted to me that he has no idea where we're going and that a gentle crash landing is a distinct possibility. We're literally going where the wind takes us.

This is my first hot air balloon flight. I've never before had the desire to be suspended far above the ground in a glorified picnic basket beneath two giant blowtorches, but it's practically
10   compulsory in Cappadocia. Even on the coldest mornings of the year, the skies are filled with around 40 similar balloons, loaded with visitors seeking an aerial perspective of this outlandish landscape. In high season, the air is crowded with up to 100.

"It's best that the balloons don't touch each other," the pilot casually informs me. "But it's hard to navigate in a hot air balloon, particularly over Cappadocia. When the sun rises, the wind
15   direction can suddenly change by 80–120 degrees; each of these valleys also channels wind, causing more uncertainty. Journeys are unchartable. Only during the final 20 minutes do we plan our landing location."

In strong winds, he tells me, we may come in to land sideways and have to adopt the brace position as we use the basket – effectively our cabin – as an anchor, allowing it to strike

20 the ground on its edge and tip over… with us inside. "It's a fun job," he says, "but a lot of responsibility."

After sinking further down, we're now teetering above – and surrounded by – treacherous spikes of volcanic rock. Despite the occasional burst of concentrated flame blasting into the balloon, we seem to be struggling to get any lift, and we instead sway between stone spikes.

25 Eventually, another jet of super-heated air – totally indistinguishable from its predecessors – arbitrarily boosts us heavenward, and I grip the basket more tightly than Yogi Bear on a pic-a-nic pilfer. In an attempt to counteract dizziness, I tie a rope handle around my wrist, take a deep breath and focus on those views – and what views.

I'd heard of what are popularly described as Cappadocia's lunar landscapes before; I agree that
30 this place is like no other on this planet.

As my balloon soars to 2,000 ft, the breadth of these wondrous views is, at last, revealed. Undulating landscapes of solidified sand dunes ripple with waved contours, like great slouching bags of hardened cement: the product of millennia-old, soft volcanic rock, sculpted by the breath of a zillion winds.

35 Below, in the Devrent Valley, the elements have whittled the limestone rock into impossible fairy-tale spires: mushroom-capped and pitted with irregular windows and doors like a movie backdrop. In other places, the rock is spiked into riotous flames; or wind-burnished into sensual, curvaceous monuments.

Thousands of years ago, labyrinthine caves were hollowed out of this yielding rock, and in the
40 second century some of the very earliest Christian churches were carved into these humble caves, dotted strangely among ancient towers formed by nature herself.

What seems like an eternity later, my pilot gently sets our basket down in a flat spot amid this aeonian landscape. Only an hour has passed. Time is indeed a matter of perspective.

---

1 At what time does the author begin his journey?

   A   Midday

   B   Sunset

   C   Late afternoon

   D   Sunrise

   E   We do not know

2 What impact does the wind have on hot air balloon navigation?

   A   It has a negligible effect.

   B   It has no effect.

   C   It has a significant effect.

   D   It has occasional effect.

   E   It has less effect than the sun.

Questions continue on next page

(3) Which of the following can govern wind direction?

    A   The sunrise and valleys

    B   Valleys and clouds

    C   The nature of the sand below

    D   The direction of the pilot's steering

    E   None of the above

(4) How does the hot air balloon pilot describe his job?

    A   It is very risky and hazardous.

    B   It is enjoyable but a lot of responsibility.

    C   It is boring but well paid.

    D   It is dull and tedious.

    E   It is exciting with little responsibility.

(5) To which other place does the author compare Cappadocia's landscape?

    A   The Kalahari desert

    B   The Arctic landscape

    C   The surface of the moon

    D   The Amazon jungle

    E   He states that it is incomparable to any other place.

(6) '…like great slouching bags of hardened cement…' (lines 32–33)

What does this phrase refer to?

    A   The heavy bags carried by the tourists

    B   The baskets of the hot air balloons

    C   The cement from the factories in the region

    D   The volcanoes that are erupting all around

    E   The sprawling masses of solidified sand dunes

(7) Which of these statements is true?

    A   The winds have taken thousands of years to carve out the landscape.

    B   The winds carved out the landscape in only a few decades.

    C   Volcanic rock is not present in Cappadocia.

    D   Lunar landscapes do not attract tourists.

    E   Only a couple of hot air balloons fly over Cappadocia each day.

8 How does the author feel about the balloon ride?

A   He is anxious but thrilled at the sight below.

B   He is fearless and adventurous.

C   He is nervous and not keen on the landscape below.

D   He wants to return to the ground as soon as possible.

E   He is afraid and wants to turn back.

9 '…the sun is peeping over the mountainous horizon.' (line 1)

Which of these words is an adjective?

A   Peeping

B   Over

C   Horizon

D   Mountainous

E   Sun

10 What is a synonym of the word 'soars'? (line 31)

A   Plummets

B   Ascends

C   Descends

D   Floats

E   Ploughs

Test	Spelling
22	You have 6 minutes to complete this test.
	You have 12 questions to complete within the time given.

In each question, circle the letter below the group of words containing a spelling mistake.

If there is no mistake, circle the letter **N**.

EXAMPLE

The peeple at the festival enjoyed the party atmosphere as the moon rose high overhead.

Ⓐ   B   C   D   N

---

① The controversy surounding the circumstances of the attack failed to subside.

A   B   C   D   N

② The artist specialised in transforming his dreams into phisycal representations.

A   B   C   D   N

③ David's apparent lack of sympathy for his opponent was criticised by the jornalist.

A   B   C   D   N

④ The queue for tickets for the concert snaked all the way around the back of the building.

A   B   C   D   N

⑤ Most of the protesters blamed the goverment for failing to act swiftly enough.

A   B   C   D   N

⑥ The importance of signs and symbals in early societies cannot be underestimated.

A   B   C   D   N

7 Katie was the only student in the class who wanted to be a soldier when she grew up.

    A   B   C   D   **N**

8 The poet detested writing verse that rhimed and so she avoided it at all costs.

    A   B   C   D   **N**

9 Whales are able to quickly identify relevent sounds made by other whales in the ocean.

    A   B   C   D   **N**

10 The shear variety of sights, sounds and colours in India is simply astonishing.

    A   B   C   D   **N**

11 The entrepreneur stated that his conscience would not allow him to complete the deal.

    A   B   C   D   **N**

12 Crying tears of joy, the conductor sinceerly and profusely thanked the audience.

    A   B   C   D   **N**

Score: .... / 12

Punctuation

In each question, circle the letter below the group of words containing a punctuation mistake.

If there is no mistake, circle the letter **N**.

EXAMPLE

The fireworks reflected in the thames to produce a brilliant and colourful display.

    A   **B**   C   D   **N**

---

1 I can't believe you're doing this There are much better solutions to this problem.

    A   B   C   D   **N**

2 The rain cloud gradually covered the entire town; growing larger and larger.

    A   B   C   D   **N**

3 I think shed rather not get involved in this dispute as it doesn't concern her.

    A   B   C   D   **N**

4 The boys' father, Edgar was known in the village as an honest and upright citizen.

    A   B   C   D   **N**

5 "I have made up my mind and you can't change it now" declared Paula.

    A   B   C   D   **N**

6 Tom didn't win the race. Nevertheless he was content with his performance.

    A   B   C   D   **N**

7 Bags of rice, sacks of potatoes and baskets of cauliflowers were transported to the Town.

    A   B   C   D   N

8 The sun set over the banks of the River as the swallows chirped cheerfully.

    A   B   C   D   N

9 All of the students' had arrived late but only one was punished by the cruel teacher.

    A   B   C   D   N

10 If Joe managed to pass the exam his father promised to buy him a new game.

    A   B   C   D   N

11 The colour-blind dog couldn't differentiate between the red, blue, and green shades.

    A   B   C   D   N

12 All of her delicately constructed decorations were suddenly, lying in ruins.

    A   B   C D   N

Sentence Completion

You have 6 minutes to complete this test.

You have 12 questions to complete within the time given.

In each question, circle the letter below the word or group of words that most accurately completes the passage.

EXAMPLE

Finding a replacement | **change** | **chart** | **chance** | **charge** | **charger** | for her phone wasn't easy.
            A   B   C   D   (E)

---

① Although he couldn't put his finger | **in** | **with** | **below** | **for** | **on** | it, Noah knew
                                          A   B   C   D   E

something was wrong.

② If I | **had known** | **was knowing** | **had been knowing** | **have known** | **know**
          A   B   C   D   E

you would waste the money, I would not have given it to you.

③ They found him | **having swang** | **swung** | **swinged** | **swing** | **swinging** | from a tree
                     A   B   C   D   E

branch that was about to snap.

④ The sloth appeared | **for** | **in** | **with** | **up** | **to** | be resting but it was quite difficult to tell.
                         A   B   C   D   E

⑤ Samantha immediately turned | **on** | **against** | **to** | **with** | **around** | her friends for
                                   A   B   C   D   E

help when she was in trouble.

6) There | wasn't | were | was | is | werent | many possible explanations for the
           A   **B**   **C**   **D**   **E**

bizarre set of circumstances.

7) The red fox was distinct from the others, not just | by | with | in | on | from | colour,
                   A   **B**   **C**   **D**   **E**

but also in behaviour.

8) Veronica | swum | had swam | had swum | swim | swimmed | from Dover to
        A   **B**   **C**   **D**   **E**

Calais: a most impressive achievement.

9) A | shoal | pride | school | gaggle | herd | of buffaloes descended down the hill in
    A   **B**   **C**   **D**   **E**

a crazed frenzy.

10) "He | oughtn't | oughtnt | oughted | should of not | should of | to have told you
       A   **B**   **C**   **D**   **E**

that," conceded the fireman.

11) The prisoner of war longed | in | by | around | for | from | his freedom, friends
                 A   **B**   **C**   **D**   **E**

and family.

12) Betty thought that the piece of music was different | from | in | by | with | about |
                         A   **B** **C**   **D**   **E**

anything she had previously heard.

Score: .... / 12

Test	# Comprehension
25	You have 10 minutes to complete this test.
	You have 10 questions to complete within the time given.

Read the passage and answer the questions that follow. In each question, circle the letter next to the correct answer.

EXAMPLE

Adam applauded the diver as she stepped onto the podium to collect her Olympic silver medal.

In which sport did the athlete compete?

A Rowing

B Gymnastics

C Hockey

(D) Diving

E Football

The following is an extract from 'Two Little Soldiers' by Guy de Maupassant

Every Sunday, as soon as they were free, the little soldiers would go for a walk. They turned to the right on leaving the barracks, crossed Courbevoie with rapid strides, as though on a forced march; then, as the houses grew scarcer, they slowed down and followed the dusty road which leads to Bezons.

5 They were small and thin, lost in their ill-fitting capes, too large and too long, whose sleeves covered their hands; their ample red trousers fell in folds around their ankles. Under the high, stiff shako one could just barely perceive two thin, hollow-cheeked Breton faces, with their calm, naïve blue eyes. They never spoke during their journey, going straight before them, the same idea in each one's mind taking the place of conversation. For at the entrance of the little

10 forest of Champioux they had found a spot which reminded them of home, and they did not feel happy anywhere else.

At the crossing of the Colombes and Chatou roads, when they arrived under the trees, they would take off their heavy, oppressive headgear and wipe their foreheads.

They always stopped for a while on the bridge at Bezons, and looked at the Seine. They

15 stood there several minutes, bending over the railing, watching the white sails, which perhaps reminded them of their home, and of the fishing smacks leaving for the open.

As soon as they had crossed the Seine, they would purchase provisions at the delicatessen, the baker's, and the wine merchant's. A piece of bologna, four cents' worth of bread, and a quart of wine, made up the luncheon which they carried away, wrapped up in their handkerchiefs. But as soon as they were out of the village their gait would slacken and they would begin to talk.

Before them was a plain with a few clumps of trees, which led to the woods, a little forest which seemed to remind them of that other forest at Kermarivan. The wheat and oat fields bordered on the narrow path, and Jean Kerderen said each time to Luc Le Ganidec:

"It's just like home, just like Plounivon."

"Yes, it's just like home."

And they went on, side by side, their minds full of dim memories of home. They saw the fields, the hedges, the forests, and beaches.

Each time they stopped near a large stone on the edge of the private estate, because it reminded them of the dolmen of Locneuven.

As soon as they reached the first clump of trees, Luc Le Ganidec would cut off a small stick, and, whittling it slowly, would walk on, thinking of the folks at home.

Jean Kerderen carried the provisions.

From time to time Luc would mention a name, or allude to some boyish prank which would give them food for plenty of thought. And the home country, so dear and so distant, would little by little gain possession of their minds, sending them back through space, to the well-known forms and noises, to the familiar scenery, with the fragrance of its green fields and sea air. They no longer noticed the smells of the city. And in their dreams they saw their friends leaving, perhaps forever, for the dangerous fishing grounds.

They were walking slowly, Luc Le Ganidec and Jean Kerderen, contented and sad, haunted by a sweet sorrow, the slow and penetrating sorrow of a captive animal which remembers the days of its freedom.

And when Luc had finished whittling his stick, they came to a little nook, where every Sunday they took their meal. They found the two bricks, which they had hidden in a hedge, and they made a little fire of dry branches and roasted their sausages on the ends of their knives.

When their last crumb of bread had been eaten and the last drop of wine had been drunk, they stretched themselves out on the grass side by side, without speaking, their half-closed eyes looking away in the distance, their hands clasped as in prayer, their red-trousered legs mingling with the bright colours of the wild flowers.

Towards noon they glanced, from time to time, towards the village of Bezons, for the dairy maid would soon be coming. Every Sunday she would pass in front of them on the way to milk her cow, the only cow in the neighborhood which was sent out to pasture.

Soon they would see the girl, coming through the fields, and it pleased them to watch the sparkling sunbeams reflected from her shining pail. They never spoke of her. They were just glad to see her, without understanding why.

Questions start on next page

1. Which word best describes the physical appearance of the two men?

   A   Gaunt

   B   Elegant

   C   Bawdy

   D   Plump

   E   Dashing

2. Which of these words best describes the colour of the two men's trousers?

   A   Turquoise

   B   Crimson

   C   Amber

   D   Silver

   E   Gold

3. Why did the two men leave their barracks every Sunday?

   A   They wanted to go to a place that reminded them of home.

   B   They were ordered to leave by their commanding officer.

   C   They had to run errands for their fellow soldiers.

   D   They wanted to go and meet their friends.

   E   They wanted to get some fresh air.

4. What did the two men stop to look at in Bezons?

   A   A fight that was taking place in the street

   B   A baker preparing fresh bread

   C   A group of farmers preparing for the harvest

   D   Boats passing by on a river

   E   The sun rising over a lake

5. Where were the two men from?

   A   Courbevoie

   B   Chatou

   C   Plounivon

   D   Champioux

   E   Locneuven

6 Which words best describe the two men's state of mind in this passage?

Option 1: nostalgic

Option 2: cheerful

Option 3: furious

Option 4: melancholic

A Options 1 and 2 only

B Options 2 and 4 only

C Options 1, 2 and 4 only

D Options 1 and 4 only

E Option 3 only

7 What was the dairy maid carrying?

A A calf

B A bottle of milk

C A bucket

D A stick of butter

E She was not carrying anything

8 What type of word is 'possession'? (line 35)

A Noun

B Verb

C Preposition

D Adjective

E Pronoun

9 Which of the following is an antonym of 'oppressive'? (line 13)

A Attuned

B Dangerous

C Opponent

D Tyrannical

E Comfortable

10 Which of the following is a synonym of 'slacken'? (line 20)

A Refer

B Improve

C Relax

D Rotate

E Lack

Score: .... / 10

Spelling

In each question, circle the letter below the group of words containing a spelling mistake.

If there is no mistake, circle the letter **N**.

EXAMPLE

The peeple at the festival enjoyed the party atmosphere as the moon rose high overhead.
   Ⓐ   B   C   D   N

① The sport of scuba diving requires a lot of sophisticated and expensive equippment.
   A   B   C   D   N

② Nadine's stomach rolled as the small boat lurched violently in the stormy waves.
   A   B   C   D   N

③ The designer attempted to create a collection which coresponded with the season.
   A   B   C   D   N

④ The twelvth and thirteenth entries in the dictionary were in an incorrect order.
   A   B   C   D   N

⑤ John suffered some light bruising on his thigh but otherwise escaped unhurt.
   A   B   C   D   N

⑥ Zak wished to accompany his wife to the doctor but she preffered to go alone.
   A   B   C   D   N

7 The unusual behaviour of the monkey had piqued the curiousity of the researcher.

      A   B   C   D   **N**

8 The winner of the lottery understandably wished to keep his identity consealed.

      A   B   C   D   **N**

9 Foreign investment poured into the country following the sucessful election.

      A   B   C   D   **N**

10 Most of the bikers had used their vehicles to block acess to the pedestrian area.

      A   B   C   D   **N**

11 The young girl implored her parents to let her take advantage of the rare opportunity.

      A   B   C   D   **N**

12 The architect was very determined to deliver the project on time and under budget.

      A   B   C   D   **N**

Score: .... / 12

Punctuation

In each question, circle the letter below the group of words containing a punctuation mistake.

If there is no mistake, circle the letter **N**.

EXAMPLE

The fireworks reflected in the thames to produce a brilliant and colourful display.

A   (B)   C   D   **N**

---

① The young doctor was exhausted; She hadn't stopped working since she had arrived.

A   B   C   D   **N**

② Dan slowly approached the small, fox that was digging energetically in his garden.

A   B   C   D   **N**

③ "Im afraid there's very little I can do to help," admitted the dejected officer.

A   B   C   D   **N**

④ The tiger – who had been captured last week – prowled around the enclosure in a rage.

A   B   C   D   **N**

⑤ Rowena did not wish to pay more than 1.50£ for the pint of milk but she had little choice.

A   B   C   D   **N**

⑥ Jill went to the supermarket and bought eggs, flour and butter to make a cake

A   B   C   D   **N**

7. Several of the volunteers were displeased with her rude, and erratic behaviour.

      A   B   C   D   **N**

8. Fiona searched her whole house for her ticket, but it was nowhere to be found.

      A   B   C   D   **N**

9. Very few of the graduates wanted to work as Scientists; they preferred engineering.

      A   B   C   D   **N**

10. All students must report to Madame Sanders (Class 4) to register for the event.

      A   B   C   D   **N**

11. Hovering above, the helicopter turned swiftly and headed towards manchester.

      A   B   C   D   **N**

12. "Hang on a minute!" called Peter. "I'll come with you so you don't need to go alone".

      A   B   C   D   **N**

Score: .... / 12

You have 6 minutes to complete this test.

You have 12 questions to complete within the time given.

In each question, circle the letter below the word or group of words that most accurately completes the passage.

EXAMPLE

Finding a replacement | change | chart | chance | charge | charger | for her phone wasn't easy.

              A   B   C   D   (E)

---

① Felix was the | most good | more better | best | gooder | bestest | mathematician

                 A   B   C   D   E

in his class at school.

② The athlete was urged by his coach not to dwell | within | in | upon | around | before |

                                        A   B   C   D   E

his recent loss.

③ | Because | For | Despite | Moreover | Even | the setback, the construction team

   A   B   C   D   E

was on track to complete the project on time.

④ | Whether | Weather | Where | With | When | you like it or not, the new system

   A   B   C   D   E

is permanent and cannot change.

⑤ | Fryer | Having fried | Fried | Frying | Fry | an egg is very simple and does not

   A   B   C   D   E

require any specialist culinary skills.

6) I think this cake is tastier | **then** | **as** | **more** | **those** | **than** | the previous one
           A **B**   **C** **D** **E**

that you baked.

7) The presenter was forced to apologise | **on** | **for** | **with** | **behalf** | **of** | the reporter's
               A **B** **C** **D** **E**

rude outburst.

8) Kevin quickly brushed his teeth before | **rush** | **rushing** | **rushed** | **having rushed**
               A **B**   **C**   **D**

| **rushes** | down the stairs.
  E

9) This brown lead belongs to my two | **boys's** | **boy's** | **boy** | **boys** | **boys'** | puppy.
             A **B** **C** **D** **E**

10) Learning to | **flyer** | **flew** | **flown** | **flight** | **fly** | an aeroplane requires time, patience
       A   **B** **C**   **D** **E**

and nerves of steel.

11) The courtier | **were** | **with** | **was** | **where** | **wear** | summoned to the palace and asked
        A **B** **C**   **D** **E**

to resign.

12) The painting depicted a girl standing in the midst | **about** | **in** | **for** | **below** | **of**
                    A **B** **C** **D** **E**

tall willow trees.

Score: .... / 12

71

Spelling

You have 6 minutes to complete this test.

You have 12 questions to complete within the time given.

In each question, circle the letter below the group of words containing a spelling mistake.

If there is no mistake, circle the letter **N**.

EXAMPLE

The peeple at the festival enjoyed the party atmosphere as the moon rose high overhead.

(A)   B   C   D   N

1. Henry's constant wailing, pleading and complaining failed to achieve the desired affect.

    A   B   C   D   N

2. The maverick scientist had developed a revolotionary cure for a rare form of cancer.

    A   B   C   D   N

3. Bridget exceled at languages and mathematics, but struggled with other subjects.

    A   B   C   D   N

4. Immediately after handing in his resignation, Daniel went to have a drink with his friends.

    A   B   C   D   N

5. The athlete pulled a muscle in the warm-up and was therefore unable to participate.

    A   B   C   D   N

6. Zara finally acomplished her dream of purchasing a yacht to sail around the world.

    A   B   C   D   N

(7) One of the most helpful books you can use when learning a new language is a dictionery.

| A | B | C | D | N |

(8) Each member of the team was a skilled individual but they did not gel well together.

| A | B | C | D | N |

(9) Ruth's impressive achievements definately helped convince those who had doubted her.

| A | B | C | D | N |

(10) The board members were alltogether dissatisfied with the executive's performance.

| A | B | C | D | N |

(11) The bees in the colony systematically polinated every flower within a mile radius.

| A | B | C | D | N |

(12) Landing an aircraft is a tricky task, especially in adverse weather conditions.

| A | B | C | D | N |

Score: .... / 12

Notes

Answers

Test 1 Comprehension

Q1   *C*   *Gloomy and still*

'We had started under a sky overcast but calm. There was no fear of heat, none of disastrous rain.'

Q2   *C*   *He felt involved*

'I was beginning to take a real share in the enterprise.'

Q3   *D*   *The guide*

'Hans, as a guide should do, moved steadily on…'

Q4   *A*   *He leads and moves on at a steady and regular pace.*

'Hans, as a guide should do, moved steadily on, keeping ahead of us at an even, smooth, and rapid pace.'

Q5   *B*   *They were robust and trained to cover all terrain.*

'The baggage horses followed him without giving any trouble.'

Q6   *D*   *Iceland had a small population.*

'Iceland is one of the largest islands in Europe. Its surface is 14,000 square miles, and it contains but 16,000 inhabitants.'

Q7   *C*   *It was very sparse.*

'Often these chains of barren rocks made a dip towards the sea, and encroached upon the scanty vegetation.'

Q8   *D*   *Disproportioned*

'I could not help smiling to see so tall a man on so small a pony, and as his long legs nearly touched the ground he looked like a six-legged centaur.'

Q9   *A*   *Simile*

Q10   *A*   *Quibble*

Test 2 Spelling

Q1   *C*   *accommodate*

Q2   *D*   *bargain*

Q3   *N*

Q4   *A*   *failed*

Q5   *A*   *mischievous*

Q6   *B*   *desperately*

Q7   *B*   *sacrifice*

Q8   *C*   *accelerated*

Q9   *N*

Q10   *N*

Q11   *C*   *guarantee*

Q12   *D*   *responsibility*

Test 3 Punctuation

Q1   *A*   *couldn't*

Q2   *C*   *cousins*

Q3   *C*   *me?"*

Q4   *A*   *Fortitude, grit*

Q5   *C*   *Paris*

Q6   *N*

Q7   *B*   *boiled eggs*

Q8   *N*

Q9   *C*   *funeral. Many OR funeral; many*

Q10   *D*   *at.*

Q11   *D*   *establishment."*

Q12   *B*   *However, Paul*

Test 4 Sentence Completion

Q1   *B*   *to*

Q2   *B*   *There*

Q3   *C*   *on*

Q4   *D*   *had*

Q5   *C*   *However*

Q6   *A*   *would*

Q7   *A*   *whose*

Q8   *B*   *must*

Q9   *B*   *over*

Q10   *D*   *of*

Q11   *E*   *her*

Q12   *E*   *up*

Test 5 Comprehension

Q1   *A*   *Cornwall*

The poem is called 'Cornish Cliffs'.

Q2   *A*   *A whale making noise in the distance*

Whales have blow-holes.

Q3   *A*   *Historical*

The poet talks about how old the fort and gun-emplacement may be.

Q4   *A*   *The horizon*

The poet is describing the meeting of the sea and the air in the distance, which is the horizon.

Test 5 answers continue on next page

Q5 **D** *Spring*

'Waft out to sea the freshness of the spring'

Q6 **B** *Sea birds*

*'The wideness which the lark-song gives the sky
Shrinks at the clang of sea-birds sailing by
Whose notes are tuned to days when seas are high.'*

Q7 **B** *Slate cottages with sycamore trees between them.*

*'Leads inland to a usual Cornish scene-
Slate cottages with sycamore between'*

Q8 **A** *'Two chapels built for half a hundred souls.'*

The line suggests there are only 50 people living in the area.

Q9 **C** *perpetual*

Q10 **E** *before*

Test 6 Spelling

Q1 **D** *convenience*

Q2 **A** *secretary*

Q3 **B** *languages*

Q4 **C** *rhythm*

Q5 **D** *Communications*

Q6 **N**

Q7 **D** *hindrance*

Q8 **A** *streaked*

Q9 **A** *occupied*

Q10 **N**

Q11 **D** *disastrous*

Q12 **N**

Test 7 Punctuation

Q1 **D** *writers and designers*

Q2 **D** *so, please*

Q3 **D** *quickly!"*

Q4 **C** *and the lows*

Q5 **D** *creation, spinach OR creation: spinach OR creation - spinach*

Q6 **N**

Q7 **A** *Peterson, the*

Q8 **C** *Bootles*

Q9 **A** *"No!" implored*

Q10 **N**

Q11 **B** *north*

Q12 **C** *items: glue,*

Test 8 Sentence Completion

Q1 **D** *take*

Q2 **C** *were*

Q3 **E** *whereas*

Q4 **D** *off*

Q5 **D** *was*

Q6 **B** *have*

Q7 **C** *paid*

Q8 **A** *in*

Q9 **C** *been*

Q10 **C** *shall*

Q11 **C** *sleep*

Q12 **D** *thinks*

Test 9 Comprehension

Q1 **D** *He surrounded himself with able administrators and was known for his integrity.*

'An astute judge of talent, he surrounded himself with the most able men in the new nation.' 'He administered the government with fairness and integrity.'

Q2 **D** *James Madison*

'James Madison was one of his principal advisors.'

Q3 **E** *There was an Indian war on the north-western frontier.*

'But as Washington's first term ended, a bloody Indian war continued on the north-western frontier and this posed a great threat.'

Q4 **B** *New political parties started to mushroom.*

'Many men in the new government…were opposed to Hamilton's financial programme. Washington despised political bias but could do little to slow the development of political parties.'

Q5 **A** *He longed to go back home but his aides persuaded him to pursue a second term.*

'Convinced that the government could get along without him, he planned to step down at the end of his first term. But his cabinet members convinced him that he alone could command the respect of members of both budding political parties.'

Q6 **C** *An international crisis shattered the economy and finances of the country because of disruption in trade and commerce.*

'The outbreak of a general European war in 1793 forced the crisis to the centre of American politics. War would be disastrous for commerce and shatter the nation's finances.'

Q7 **C** *It was affected by foreign affairs.*

'Although Washington's department heads agreed that the United States should remain neutral, disagreements over foreign policy provoked tensions among them.'

Q8 *E* *Biography*

Biography focuses on describing the lives of specific people.

Q9 *C* *Common nouns*

Q10 *A* *Marked*

Test 10 Spelling

Q1 *C* *awkward*

Q2 *N*

Q3 *D* *existence*

Q4 *B* *privilege*

Q5 *D* *cemetery*

Q6 *B* *pronunciation*

Q7 *N*

Q8 *A* *exaggerated*

Q9 *N*

Q10 *D* *environmental*

Q11 *N*

Q12 *C* *appreciate*

Test 11 Punctuation

Q1 *C* *summer*

Q2 *A* *whiskers*

Q3 *C* *It's*

Q4 *D* *o'clock*

Q5 *D* *That's*

Q6 *C* *cook and*

Q7 *B* *clothes*

Q8 *C* *Wednesday*

Q9 *B* *"Can*

Q10 *N*

Q11 *D* *square.*

Q12 *D* *'The*

Test 12 Sentence Completion

Q1 *C* *went*

Q2 *A* *with*

Q3 *D* *which*

Q4 *A* *are*

Q5 *D* *that*

Q6 *B* *We're*

Q7 *C* *as*

Q8 *D* *theirs*

Q9 *E* *stand*

Q10 *A* *to*

Q11 *D* *implored*

Q12 *B* *of*

Test 13 Comprehension

Q1 *E* *They viewed dragons as an enemy.*

'There are no dragons today – mainly thanks to the knights and heroes who so thoughtlessly rode about the place killing them off.'

Q2 *C* *They hissed smoke out of their nostrils.*

'When they were angry or frightened, smoke would come hissing out of their nostrils.'

Q3 *D* *Dragons were believed to have caused drought and famine in China.*

'A dragon guarded the houses of the Chinese gods and brought rain to the earth when the crops needed it.'

Q4 *A* *They mainly treat dragons as symbolic or figurative creatures.*

'…carried westward, it …has been transformed more recently into a purely allegorical figure.'

Q5 *A* *Plants and animals*

'…the early Chinese believed that certain species of animals or plants possessed the power to overcome nature's fury.'

Q6 *C* *A sacred symbol or icon that was thought to bring good fortune.*

'Different tribes regarded a particular animal or plant as their totem, a tribe's special guardian able to provide food and avert disaster through omens or signs.'

Q7 *D* *To carve out the terrain of China.*

'…and an emerald-scaled dragon whose wings he used to sculpt the land.'

Q8 *B* *The dragon, phoenix, tortoise and unicorn*

The final paragraph references these four creatures. (lines 37–39)

Q9 *C* *Protector*

Q10 *D* *In addition to other things*

Test 14 Spelling

Q1 *A* *programme*

Q2 *A* *recommended*

Q3 *B* *restaurant*

Q4 *N*

Q5 *N*

Q6 *D* *aggrieved*

Q7 *B* *explanation*

Test 14 answers continue on next page

Q8 **B** lightning

Q9 **A** Occasionally

Q10 **C** sufficiently

Q11 **B** aggressive

Q12 **A** practised

Test 15 Punctuation

Q1 **A** hadn't

Q2 **C** green

Q3 **C** ear,

Q4 **D** larger, square-shaped

Q5 **N**

Q6 **B** breath, looked

Q7 **N**

Q8 **N**

Q9 **C** well, received

Q10 **N**

Q11 **C** University

Q12 **C** Eve

Test 16 Sentence Completion

Q1 **A** known

Q2 **D** on

Q3 **C** no

Q4 **D** had been waiting

Q5 **A** so

Q6 **B** coldest

Q7 **A** Pick

Q8 **E** Since

Q9 **E** on

Q10 **B** hungrily

Q11 **A** should have

Q12 **B** to

Test 17 Comprehension

Q1 **D** It was hot and humid.

'You must imagine a hot and humid place…'

Q2 **B** 'The riot of flowers is incessant.'

This quote suggests that there were lots of flowers in the zoo.

Q3 **A** Plants

Jacarandas are mentioned in a list of trees and shrubs, so you can deduce that they must also be plants.

Q4 **A** The shrill cries of birds

'…only outdone in volume by the shrill cries of strange birds.'

Q5 **D** It was a barrier to prevent entry to the zoo without payment.

'You come to a turnstile. You distractedly pay a small sum of money.'

Q6 **A** The author had fond memories of his time at the zoo.

The author enjoyed his time at the zoo as a child and so he described it with this positive phrase: 'I have nothing but the fondest memories of growing up in a zoo.'

Q7 **B** They roared every morning.

'…the lions could be counted upon to roar their heads off between five-thirty and six every morning.'

Q8 **E** Seals

All the other animals are mentioned as being seen in the morning.

Q9 **C** Extremely angry

Q10 **A** Kind regard

Test 18 Spelling

Q1 **A** competition

Q2 **D** leisure

Q3 **A** Parliament

Q4 **A** According

Q5 **B** profession

Q6 **N**

Q7 **N**

Q8 **N**

Q9 **N**

Q10 **A** communities

Q11 **B** persuade

Q12 **D** vegetables

Test 19 Punctuation

Q1 **N**

Q2 **N**

Q3 **D** you're

Q4 **B** eyes,

Q5 **N**

Q6 **B** homework,

Q7 **A** They're

Q8 **C** polished, gleaming

Q9 **D** it's

Q10 **A** Woodstock

Q11 *C* behaviour,"

Q12 *B* west

Test 20 Sentence Completion

Q1 *D* whirring

Q2 *E* Weren't

Q3 *D* for

Q4 *E* notice

Q5 *A* feel about

Q6 *C* whichever

Q7 *D* earlier

Q8 *B* leant

Q9 *E* for

Q10 *B* of

Q11 *A* promptly

Q12 *D* If

Test 21 Comprehension

Q1 *D* Sunrise

'It's a frosty 6 am and the sun is peeping over the mountainous horizon.'

Q2 *C* It has a significant effect.

'We're literally going where the wind takes us.'

Q3 *A* The sunrise and valleys

'When the sun rises, the wind direction can suddenly change by 80–120 degrees; each of these valleys also channels wind, causing more uncertainty.'

Q4 *B* It is enjoyable but a lot of responsibility.

"It's a fun job," he says, "but a lot of responsibility."

Q5 *C* The surface of the moon

'I'd heard of what are popularly described as Cappadocia's lunar landscapes before; I agree that this place is like no other on this planet.'

Q6 *E* The sprawling masses of solidified sand dunes

'Undulating landscapes of solidified sand dunes ripple with waved contours, like great slouching bags of hardened cement…'

Q7 *A* The winds have taken thousands of years to carve out the landscape.

'…the product of millennia-old, soft volcanic rock, sculpted by the breath of a zillion winds.'

Q8 *A* He is anxious but thrilled at the sight below.

The author highlights the perilous nature of the journey but also praises the beautiful landscape.

Q9 *D* Mountainous

Q10 *B* Ascends

Test 22 Spelling

Q1 *A* surrounding

Q2 *D* physical

Q3 *D* journalist

Q4 *N*

Q5 *B* government

Q6 *B* symbols

Q7 *N*

Q8 *C* rhymed

Q9 *C* relevant

Q10 *A* sheer

Q11 *N*

Q12 *B* sincerely

Test 23 Punctuation

Q1 *B* this. There

Q2 *C* town,

Q3 *A* she'd

Q4 *B* Edgar,

Q5 *D* now,"

Q6 *B* Nevertheless,

Q7 *D* town

Q8 *B* river

Q9 *A* students

Q10 *B* exam,

Q11 *D* blue and

Q12 *C* suddenly lying

Test 24 Sentence Completion

Q1 *E* on

Q2 *A* had known

Q3 *E* swinging

Q4 *E* to

Q5 *C* to

Q6 *B* were

Q7 *C* in

Q8 *C* had swum

Q9 *E* herd

Q10 *A* oughtn't

Q11 *D* for

Q12 *A* from

Test 25 Comprehension

Q1 **A** *Gaunt*

'They were small and thin, lost in their ill-fitting capes, too large and too long...'

Q2 **B** *Crimson*

'their ample red trousers'

Q3 **A** *They wanted to go to a place that reminded them of home.*

'For at the entrance of the little forest of Champioux they had found a spot which reminded them of home, and they did not feel happy anywhere else.'

Q4 **D** *Boats passing by on a river*

'They always stopped for a while on the bridge at Bezons, and looked at the Seine. They stood there several minutes, bending over the railing, watching the white sails, which perhaps reminded them of their home, and of the fishing smacks leaving for the open.'

Q5 **C** *Plounivon*

"It's just like home, just like Plounivon."

Q6 **D** *Options 1 and 4 only*

'They were walking slowly, Luc Le Ganidec and Jean Kerderen, contented and sad, haunted by a sweet sorrow, the slow and penetrating sorrow of a captive animal which remembers the days of its freedom.'

Q7 **C** *A bucket*

'...from her shining pail.'

Q8 **A** *Noun*

Q9 **E** *Comfortable*

Q10 **C** *Relax*

Test 26 Spelling

Q1 **D** *equipment*

Q2 **N**

Q3 **C** *corresponded*

Q4 **A** *twelfth*

Q5 **N**

Q6 **D** *preferred*

Q7 **C** *curiosity*

Q8 **D** *concealed*

Q9 **D** *successful*

Q10 **D** *access*

Q11 **N**

Q12 **N**

Test 27 Punctuation

Q1 **B** *; she OR . She*

Q2 **B** *small fox*

Q3 **A** *"I'm*

Q4 **N**

Q5 **C** *£1.50*

Q6 **D** *cake.*

Q7 **C** *rude and*

Q8 **N**

Q9 **C** *scientists*

Q10 **N**

Q11 **D** *Manchester*

Q12 **D** *alone."*

Test 28 Sentence Completion

Q1 **C** *best*

Q2 **C** *upon*

Q3 **C** *Despite*

Q4 **A** *Whether*

Q5 **D** *Frying*

Q6 **E** *than*

Q7 **B** *for*

Q8 **B** *rushing*

Q9 **E** *boys'*

Q10 **E** *fly*

Q11 **C** *was*

Q12 **E** *of*

Test 29 Spelling

Q1 **D** *effect*

Q2 **C** *revolutionary*

Q3 **A** *excelled*

Q4 **N**

Q5 **N**

Q6 **B** *accomplished*

Q7 **D** *dictionary*

Q8 **N**

Q9 **B** *definitely*

Q10 **B** *altogether*

Q11 **C** *pollinated*

Q12 **N**